Is it Safe?

An Issue that Divides the Evangelical World

Geoff Barnard

Abbreviations:

ASV = American Standard Version
NIV = New International Version
KJV = King James Version
NKJV = New King James Version
RSV = Revised Standard Version
NRSV = New Revised Standard Version

ISBN 978-965-7542-42-2

This book can be ordered by contacting:

Author's e-mail: gjrb2@aol.com

or

E-mail: tsurtsinapublications@gmail.com
Website: www.lulu.com

A Tsur Tsina Publication

Is it Safe?

Geoff Barnard

CONTENTS

Is it Safe?   5

Repetitive Nature of Biblical Prophecy   10

Prophecies in Zechariah 12 through 14   12

Initial Fulfilment of Zechariah's Prophecy   19

The Final Conflict   24

Israel's return to the Land   26

Israel are Lost Sheep   27

Israel Returns to the Land out of Holocaust   31

Valley of the Dry Bones   43

Israel Returns to the Land in Unbelief   45

If Israel is not Safe, We can be Certain of Nothing   46

Is Israel the Only Safe Place for the Jewish People?   46

Is Anywhere else Safe?   48

So will Anywhere be Safe?   50

Appendix 1: Holocaust   52

Appendix 2: The Final Battle   54

Is it Safe?[1]

There are two radically differing views about the future of Israel. This is true even in those Christian circles that accept that Israel has a part to play in God's eternal purposes for the world. Obviously, those holding to a replacement theological position will only see the current modern state of Israel as a political anomaly. As we will see, the two radically differing views regarding the future welfare of modern Israel are also expressed within the Messianic community even within the Land itself.

The first view suggests that modern Israel is destined for judgment, a view that most replacement theologians hold. Remarkably, many Messianic teachers such as Arnold Fruchtenbaum[2] and, in particular, Art Katz[3] represent this position. It is also possible that many within evangelistic organizations such as "*Jews for Jesus*" may hold to this view. Motivation for evangelism (which is commendable) is the deeply held belief that it is only in Jesus that safety can be found. Modern Israel is seen as a secular state and cannot be the fulfillment of such verses as:

Jeremiah 23:5-6 (NIV) "*The days are coming," declares the LORD, "when I will raise up to David a righteous Branch, a King who will reign wisely and do what is just and right in the land. In his days Judah will be saved and Israel will live in safety. This is the name by which he will be called: The LORD Our Righteousness.*

---

[1] This title is inspired by an amazing and terrifying scene in a film called "Marathon Man" where Laurence Olivier, who plays a Nazi dentist, has Dustin Hoffman (a Jew) strapped and helpless in a chair. He repeats the words "Is it safe?" several times with a slightly different intonation with each statement. The Dustin Hoffman character has no idea what the Nazi is getting at and because of that, he suffers at the dentist's hands.

[2] Fruchtenbaum AG (2005) The Modern State of Israel in Bible Prophecy. www.arielm.org/dcs/pdf/mbs189m.pdf

[3] http://artkatzministries.org/articles/the-necessary-death-and-resurrection-of-israel/

*__Jeremiah 23:7-8 (NIV)__ "So then, the days are coming,"
declares the LORD, "when people will no longer say, 'As
surely as the LORD lives, who brought the Israelites up out
of Egypt,' but they will say, 'As surely as the LORD lives,
who brought the descendants of Israel up out of the land of
the north and out of all the countries where he had banished
them.' Then they will live in their own land."*

Jesus is the Lord our Righteousness. Probably, most
Christian believers are agreed on this. Are these his days?
If they are not, and Israel is not a believing nation at the
present time, then an argument could be made that modern
Israel is not yet safe. Israel is also a sinful nation. In
particular, the state has one of the most liberal abortion
policies of any nation. It is possible that as many children
have died through abortion in Israel as those that died in
the Holocaust. How can God overlook this?

It is implicit in this argument that modern Israel must face
further judgment and the current situation in the Middle East
is presumably setting the scene for this. This might also be
the reason why so many Messianic Jews (and Orthodox
Jews for that matter), particularly in North America,
seemingly have no desire to make Aliyah. Their reasons
might be that they believe that they are safer in the USA
than they would be in the Middle East.

The situation among orthodox Jewry is also very significant.
Many, even within Israel, do not recognize the state as
being legitimate. The belief is that only the Messiah can
establish the nation and verses such as Jeremiah 23:5-8
might seem to support this position.

For evangelical Christians (both Jew and Gentile) holding
the "Israel is not safe" view, a number of things inevitably
follow:

1. The Primacy of Jewish Evangelism

It is now increasingly urgent to preach the gospel to Jewish people. In a sense this has to be correct. With the Apostle Paul, we all agree:

Romans 1:16 (RSV) *For I am not ashamed of the gospel: it is the power of God for salvation to every one who has faith, to the Jew first and also to the Greek.*

While it is true that tens of thousands of Jewish people have become Messianic believers, particularly in the USA and in the former Soviet Union, it is still also true that in large measure (particularly among the Orthodox) that …

Romans 11:28 (NIV) *As far as the gospel is concerned, they are enemies on your account; but as far as election is concerned, they are loved on account of the patriarchs.*

2. The Lack of Support for those Ministries encouraging Aliyah

It follows that if you believe that modern Israel is destined for judgment, and maybe even destruction, you would not go out of the way to encourage Aliyah. In fact, there are evangelical ministries[4] who are very strongly opposed to other Christian organizations, such as Ebenezer, Christian Friends of Israel; Bridges for Peace; and the International Christian Embassy who are all seen as supportive of the present day Aliyah. The main objection of the critics is the stance that these pro-Aliyah ministries make regarding Jewish evangelism. There is also a strong antipathy towards spending vast sums of money bringing Jewish people into perceived danger.

---

[4] For example, Jacob Prasch, Moriel Ministries [see https://www.moriel.org/]

3. Minimizing the Significance of the Holocaust

Inevitably, and I think characteristically, holding the "Israel is not safe" position leads to minimizing the significance of the Holocaust both within the history of the Jewish people and in the purposes of God. A common feature will be the way the verses in Zechariah 13:7-9 are interpreted.[5]

We shall have occasion to look at these verses in detail but suffice to say, at this stage, that it is a very common characteristic of the "Israel is not safe" position that the Holocaust is seen simply as a foretaste of something far worse happening to the Jewish people in the days to come. In other words, *the time of Jacob's trouble* is viewed as a future prophetic event. It is, therefore, important to see these verses in Zechariah in context and also to appreciate the repetitive nature of biblical prophecy.

4. Salvation is only seen in Spiritual Terms

Jeremiah 30:7 (NIV) How awful that day will be! None will be like it. It will be a time of trouble for Jacob, but he will be saved out of it.

If salvation is seen in solely spiritual terms and since the Jewish people are to be saved out of "the time of Jacob's trouble", it has to follow that the Holocaust was not the final fulfillment of this terrible event.

---

[5] **Zechariah 13:7-9 (NIV)** Awake, O sword, against my shepherd, against the man who is close to me!" declares the LORD Almighty. "Strike the shepherd, and the sheep will be scattered, and I will turn my hand against the little ones. In the whole land," declares the LORD, "two-thirds will be struck down and perish; yet one-third will be left in it. This third I will bring into the fire; I will refine them like silver and test them like gold. They will call on my name and I will answer them; I will say, 'They are my people,' and they will say, 'The LORD is our God.'

5. The Return of Jesus

Those who hold radically differing positions regarding the status of the modern state of Israel with respect to God's purposes, almost certainly will hold differing opinions as to the prophetic events leading up to the return of Jesus.

For example, if *"the time of Jacob's trouble"* is regarded as a future event and is to be equated to *"the Great Tribulation"*, then this belief is often (although not always) associated with a secret pre-tribulation "rapture", at any time, to bring "the church age" to an end. This dispensational anticipation would shield believers from the ravages (wrath) of God who will lay waste the earth and leave the unbelievers and the Jewish people, in particular, to their fate.

This is a prevalent eschatological belief in much of the evangelical church, particularly in North America. It is this writer's opinion that this doctrine is a false deception and is anti-Semitic replacement theology of the most flagrant kind.

For an excellent overview of the history and the various doctrines of Dispensationalism, the reader is referred to:

https://en.wikipedia.org/wiki/Dispensationalism

The Repetitive Nature of Biblical Prophecy

Before we look in detail at the verses in the final chapters of Zechariah, we need to appreciate the repetitive nature of much biblical Messianic prophecy. To illustrate this concept, I wish to refer to a very well-known prophecy in Isaiah.

Isaiah 9:6-7 (NIV) For to us a child is born, to us a son is given, and the government will be on his shoulders. And he will be called Wonderful Counsellor, Mighty God, Everlasting Father, Prince of Peace. Of the increase of his government and peace there will be no end. He will reign on David's throne and over his kingdom, establishing and upholding it with justice and righteousness from that time on and forever. The zeal of the LORD Almighty will accomplish this.

These verses will be found on many Christmas cards and quite rightly so because they are fulfilled in the birth of Jesus. However, it should be noted that these famous verses, as translated in the NIV, begin with the preposition "for". The actual Hebrew word is כִּי [transliterated "ki"]. This word means "because". Consequently, the verses have to be read in their proper context which is the preceding verses, namely:

Isaiah 9:3-5 (NIV)[6] *You have enlarged the nation and increased their joy; they rejoice before you as people rejoice at the harvest, as men rejoice when dividing the plunder. For as in the day of Midian's defeat, you have shattered the yoke that burdens them, the bar across their shoulders, the rod of their oppressor. Every warrior's boot used in battle and every garment rolled in blood will be destined for burning, will be fuel for the fire. ...* **for** *[because] unto us ...*

---

[6] These verses are never included on any Christmas card or in any carol service. The Christian World has no idea what to do with them. We generally move from verse 2 (i.e. the people walking in darkness have seen a great light) directly to verse 6 (i.e. for unto us a child is born)

The initial fulfillment of these prophetic verses was the birth of Hezekiah during the dark reign of his father King Ahaz (see 2 Chronicles 28). It was during the reign of Hezekiah that the Assyrian armies were destroyed when they attacked Jerusalem.[7]

However, the birth of Hezekiah does not fulfill every aspect of the prophecy. Hezekiah died. He was not the one to reign on David's throne from that time on and forever. Many years later, the angel Gabriel brought this message to Mary who was to become the mother of Jesus.

Luke 1:32-33 (RSV) *He will be great, and will be called the Son of the Most High; and the Lord God will give to him the throne of his father David, and he will reign over the house of Jacob for ever; and of his kingdom there will be no end."*

Jesus fulfils the eternal nature of this prophetic promise. However, there is yet to be the final and total fulfillment of **all** the words in Isaiah 9:1-7 when the people of Israel, who are still walking in darkness, will see the great light. It is important to remember that Jesus will always be the Light of the World (John 8:12).

These events are described in great detail in the final chapters of Zechariah.

---

[7] **2 Kings 19:32-35 (RSV)** "Therefore thus says the LORD concerning the king of Assyria, He shall not come into this city or shoot an arrow there, or come before it with a shield or cast up a siege mound against it. By the way that he came, by the same he shall return, and he shall not come into this city, says the LORD. For I will defend this city to save it, for my own sake and for the sake of my servant David." And that night the angel of the LORD went forth, and slew a hundred and eighty-five thousand in the camp of the Assyrians; and when men arose early in the morning, behold, these were all dead bodies..

The Prophecies of Zechariah in Chapters 12 through 14

One of the characteristics of the theology of Christians holding the "Israel is not safe" position is the mistaken idea that Zechariah chapters 12 through 14 describes one event. However, the conflict described in the early verses in chapter 12 cannot be the same as the conflict described at the beginning of chapter 14 for several reasons. Let us first consider these words in chapter 12.

Zechariah 12:1-3 (NIV) This is the word of the LORD concerning Israel. The LORD, who stretches out the heavens, who lays the foundation of the earth, and who forms the spirit of man within him, declares: "I am going to make Jerusalem a cup that sends the surrounding peoples reeling. Judah will be besieged as well as Jerusalem. On that day, when all the nations of the earth are gathered against her, I will make Jerusalem an immovable rock for all the nations. All who try to move it will injure themselves.

An Immovable Rock

The focus and context of this prophecy is the status of Jerusalem when the surrounding nations are in uproar. Judah will be under siege. However, the status of Jerusalem remains inviolate. It cannot be moved and any attempt to do so will result in injury. This is explicitly stated in the following verses.

*Zechariah 12:4-6 (NIV) On that day I will strike every horse with panic and its rider with madness," declares the LORD. "**I will keep a watchful eye over the house of Judah**, but I will blind all the horses of the nations. Then the leaders of Judah will say in their hearts, 'The people of Jerusalem are strong, because the LORD Almighty is their God.' "On that day I will make the leaders of Judah like a brazier in a woodpile, like a flaming torch among sheaves. **They will consume right and left all the surrounding peoples, but Jerusalem will remain intact in her place*** [emphases added].

Whatever takes place during this event, Israel more than survives. Jerusalem remains intact (i.e. it is not divided). Moreover, the nation is enlarged (see Isaiah 9:3). Whatever nations that actually attack Israel are destroyed and this is described in the following verses.

*Zechariah 12:7-9 (NIV) "The LORD will save the dwellings of Judah first, so that the honor of the house of David and of Jerusalem's inhabitants may not be greater than that of Judah. **On that day the LORD will shield those who live in Jerusalem**, so that the feeblest among them will be like David, and the house of David will be like God, like the Angel of the LORD going before them. **On that day I will set out to destroy all the nations that attack Jerusalem*** [emphases added].

Although it is inappropriate to be completely dogmatic, it is this author's opinion that the events described in Zechariah 12:1-9 parallel the prophecies in Ezekiel chapters 38 and 39, namely the Gog and Magog conflict.[8] The outworking of the Ezekiel prophecy results in the destruction of the invaders and spiritual revival. The last words of this prophecy are:

Ezekiel 39:29 (RSV) And I will not hide my face any more from them, when I pour out my Spirit upon the house of Israel, says the Lord GOD.

This is completely paralleled in Zechariah 12.

Zechariah 12:10 (NIV) I will pour out on the house of David and the inhabitants of Jerusalem a spirit of grace and supplication. They will look on me, the one they have pierced, and they will mourn for him as one mourns for an only child, and grieve bitterly for him as one grieves for a firstborn son.

The survival of Israel during this conflict is miraculous as indeed it was during the war of Independence in 1948. However, there is also recognition that, although Israel has been strong in this conflict, the Almighty God is their God (Zechariah 12:5). But this does not explain the response when God pours out his Spirit upon the Nation.

Zechariah 12:11-14 (NIV) On that day the weeping in Jerusalem will be great, like the weeping of Hadad Rimmon in the plain of Megiddo. The land will mourn, each clan by itself, with their wives by themselves: the clan of the house of David and their wives, the clan of the house of Nathan and their wives, the clan of the house of Levi and their wives, the clan of Shimei and their wives, and all the rest of the clans and their wives.

---

[8] These chapters describe events that also may have more than one fulfillment (see, for example, Revelation 20:8)

Eyes are opened and one who was pierced will be seen. This leads to the devastating conclusion that Jesus is their promised Messiah but he has been rejected by the Nation (as a whole) for 2000 years. The weeping is **like** that which took place when King Josiah was killed in battle when he went to fight Pharaoh Neco at Megiddo. He was shot (even pierced) by arrows and carried back to Jerusalem where he died. The mourning for King Josiah was very great.[9]

I believe that this event in Zechariah 12 describes the beginning of a process that will take time. The recognition of the Messiah through the outpouring of the Holy Spirit will not lead to instantaneous change. Two thousand years of struggle, persecution and suffering will need to be re-assessed.

However,

Zechariah 13:1-2 (NIV) *On that day a fountain will be opened to the house of David and the inhabitants of Jerusalem, to cleanse them from sin and impurity. "On that day, I will banish the names of the idols from the land, and they will be remembered no more," declares the LORD Almighty. "I will remove both the prophets and the spirit of impurity from the land."*

Please note that prior to this event, there is a spirit of impurity and idolatry in the land. In other words, Israel is an imperfect and sinful people when the Spirit is poured out. They do not deserve what will happen. But that is the actual point. It is a Spirit of GRACE and supplication.

The prophet Ezekiel puts it like this:

---

[9] **2 Chronicles 35:25 (NIV)** Jeremiah composed laments for Josiah, and to this day all the men and women singers commemorate Josiah in the laments. These became a tradition in Israel and are written in the Laments.

__Ezekiel 36:22, 32 (NIV)__ "Therefore say to the house of Israel, 'This is what the Sovereign LORD says: It is not for your sake, O house of Israel, that I am going to do these things, but for the sake of my holy name, which you have profaned among the nations where you have gone … I want you to know that I am not doing this for your sake, declares the Sovereign LORD. Be ashamed and disgraced for your conduct, O house of Israel!"

and

__Ezekiel 39:26-28 (RSV)__ They shall forget their shame, and all the treachery they have practiced against me, when they dwell securely in their land with none to make them afraid, when I have brought them back from the peoples and gathered them from their enemies' lands, and through them have vindicated my holiness in the sight of many nations. Then they shall know that I am the LORD their God because I sent them into exile among the nations, and then gathered them into their own land. I will leave none of them remaining among the nations any more.

The renewal and cleansing of the people and the land will take time. Ezekiel speaks of a seven year period[10] and it is tempting to cautiously speculate that these seven years might correspond the final seven years prior to the return of Jesus which is considered in many eschatological schemes. But please note that during this period, the nation of Israel is becoming a believing and righteous nation. The times of the Gentiles will have been fulfilled and all Israel will be saved as expressed by Paul in his letter to the Romans.

---

[10] **Ezekiel 39:9 (RSV)** Then those who dwell in the cities of Israel will go forth and make fires of the weapons and burn them, shields and bucklers, bows and arrows, handpikes and spears, and they will make fires of them **for seven years** [emphasis added].

Romans 11:25-27 (KJV) *For I would not, brethren, that ye should be ignorant of this mystery, lest ye should be wise in your own conceits; that blindness in part is happened to Israel, until the fullness of the Gentiles be come in.[11] And so* **all** *Israel shall be saved: as it is written, there shall come out of Zion the Deliverer, and shall turn away ungodliness from Jacob: For this is my covenant unto them, when I shall take away their sins [emphasis added].*

And what is this covenant? It is the New Covenant that is sealed with the blood of Jesus and administered by the Holy Spirit. It is described in the book of Jeremiah.

Jeremiah 31:31 (NIV) *"The time is coming," declares the LORD, "when I will make a new covenant* **with the house of Israel and with the house of Judah***" [emphasis added].*

The final fulfillment of this covenant that began at the annual celebration of Shavuot (also known as the Feast of Weeks or Pentecost), recorded in Acts chapter 2, will be as follows:

Jeremiah 31:34 (NIV) *No longer will a man teach his neighbor, or a man his brother, saying, 'Know the LORD,'* **because they will** **all** **know me, from the least of them to the greatest***," declares the LORD. "For I will forgive their wickedness and will remember their sins no more" [emphasis added].[12]*

---

[11] The NIV translation, namely, "until the full number of the Gentiles has come in" is very unhelpful.

[12] See also **Isaiah 45:22-25 (NIV)** "Turn to me and be saved, all you ends of the earth; for I am God, and there is no other. By myself I have sworn, my mouth has uttered in all integrity a word that will not be revoked: Before me every knee will bow; by me every tongue will swear. They will say of me, 'In the LORD alone are righteousness and strength.'" All who have raged against him will come to him and be put to shame. **But in the LORD** **all** **the descendants of Israel will be found righteous and will exult** [emphasis added].

"They will look on me … and grieve bitterly for him as one grieves for a firstborn son." Zechariah 12:10 [13]

The Initial Fulfillment
of Zechariah's Prophecy

We have to appreciate that the looking on the one pierced was also fulfilled during the crucifixion of Jesus.

John 19:37 (NIV) *and, as another scripture says, "They will look on the one they have pierced."*

This is another clear example of the repetitive nature of biblical prophecy. It is interesting to note that the New Testament usage of the prophetic scriptures often takes verses out of context.[14] The crucifixion of Jesus took place during the time of the Roman occupation of Judea and in forty years, Jerusalem was to be destroyed. Accordingly, the context of Zechariah chapter 12 demands a future fulfillment when every word is set in its right context.

Another very important example is Jesus' usage of the prophecy in Zechariah chapter 13.

Zechariah 13:7 (NIV) *"Awake, O sword, against my shepherd, against the man who is close to me!" declares the LORD Almighty. "Strike the shepherd, and the sheep will be scattered, and I will turn my hand against the little ones.*

Matthew 26:31 (NIV) *Then Jesus told them, "This very night you will all fall away on account of me, for it is written: "'I will strike the shepherd, and the sheep of the flock will be scattered.'*

---

[13] Jesus in the arms of Mary - Pencil drawing by Rick Wienecke

[14] Another clear example is the use of Hosea's prophecy in Matthew's gospel (see Matthew 2:15)

It is apparent that Jesus applies these words in the prophecy of Zechariah to himself. He is, after all, the good Shepherd (Ezekiel 34:12; John 10:11). Consequently, the very next verse must have been fulfilled following that time, namely:

Zechariah 13:7-8 (NIV) *"**And** I will turn my hand against the little ones. In the whole land," declares the LORD, "two-thirds will be struck down and perish; yet one-third will be left in it [emphasis added].*

These terrible words describe the suffering of the Jewish people at the time of the destruction of Jerusalem during the Roman-Jewish wars in the first and second centuries. For example, Josephus writes that 1,100,000 Jewish people perished at the hands of the Romans in 70 CE.[15] Describing this massacre, Milman has written:

> *"The slaughter within was even more dreadful than the spectacle from without. Men and women, old and young, insurgents and priests, those who fought and those who entreated mercy, were hewn down in indiscriminate carnage. The number of the slain exceeded that of the slayers. The legionaries had to clamber over heaps of dead to carry on the work of extermination."* [16]

Jesus anticipated this and warned his disciples.

Luke 21:24 (NIV) *They will fall by the sword and will be taken as prisoners to all the nations. Jerusalem will be trampled on by the Gentiles until the times of the Gentiles are fulfilled.*[17]

---

[15] http://en.wikipedia.org/wiki/Siege_of_Jerusalem_(70)

[16] Milman HH The History of the Jews, book 16

[17] I have developed these themes in a extended study of the Olivet Discourse which is entitled "When Will These Things Be?" Please contact the author on: gjrb2@aol.com

"When you see Jerusalem being surrounded by armies, you will know that its desolation is near." (Luke 21:20) [18]

One might conclude that two-thirds of the population perished during these conflicts. Furthermore, I believe that throughout history, these terrible words may have been repeated. Maybe two-thirds of all the people of Israel have perished in the Crusades, the Inquisition, the pogroms and the massacres. Only God knows, but one thing we do know, two-thirds of European Jewry perished in the Holocaust. [19]

---

[18] The Siege and Destruction of Jerusalem by David Roberts (1850)

[19] The Holocaust (called Shoah in Hebrew) refers to the period from January 30, 1933, when Adolf Hitler became chancellor of Germany, to May 8, 1945 (V-E Day), when the war in Europe ended. During this time, Jews in Europe were subjected to progressively harsh persecution that ultimately led to the murder of 6,000,000 Jews (1.5 million of these being children) and the destruction of 5,000 Jewish communities. These deaths represented two-thirds of European Jewry and one-third of world Jewry. The Jews who died were not casualties of the fighting that ravaged Europe during World War II. Rather, they were the victims of Germany's deliberate and systematic attempt to annihilate the entire Jewish population of Europe, a plan Hitler called the "Final Solution" (Endlosung). Taken from: http://www.jewishvirtuallibrary.org/jsource/Holocaust/history.html. The reader is also referred to Appendix 1 (Page 52).

So what will be the final fulfillment of Zechariah 13:8? Has God brought the people of Israel back to the Land so that a further two-thirds will perish in yet another Holocaust? I totally reject this position. It is another expression of replacement theology and I believe it to be totally deceptive. The reasons for this are vitally important for the Christian world which is largely unprepared for what is to come.

So how can we understand this? Actually it is quite simple. It is to do with the meaning of the words translated in the NIV and in most English Bibles as "in the whole land". The words in Hebrew are:

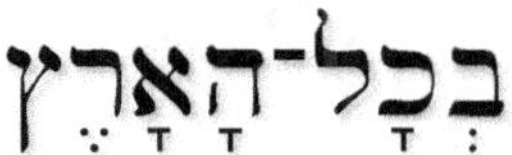

This may be transliterated "b'Kol ha-Aretz". It certainly can be translated "in the whole land" but, depending on the context, it can also be translated "in the whole earth".[20] Thus, I believe the final expression of these words will be:

Zechariah 13:8 (GB) *In the whole earth," declares the LORD, "two-thirds will be struck down and perish; yet one-third will be left in it.*

This is totally consistent with the words of Isaiah and the words of Jesus:

Isaiah 24:1-2 (RSV) *Behold, the LORD will lay waste the earth and make it desolate, and he will twist its surface and scatter its inhabitants. And it shall be, as with the people, so with the priest; as with the slave, so with his master; as with the maid, so with her mistress; as with the buyer, so with the seller; as with the lender, so with the borrower; as with the creditor, so with the debtor ...*

---

[20] In the original text, there were no vocalization marks. These were added centuries later.

***Isaiah 24:3-6 (RSV)** The earth shall be utterly laid waste and utterly despoiled; for the LORD has spoken this word. The earth mourns and withers, the world languishes and withers; the heavens languish together with the earth. The earth lies polluted under its inhabitants; for they have transgressed the laws, violated the statutes, broken the everlasting covenant. Therefore a curse devours the earth, and its inhabitants suffer for their guilt; therefore the inhabitants of the earth are scorched, and few men are left.*

Actually, there will be a third left.

***Luke 21:25-26 (NIV)** There will be signs in the sun, moon and stars. On the earth, nations will be in anguish and perplexity at the roaring and tossing of the sea. Men will faint from terror, apprehensive of what is coming on the world, for the heavenly bodies will be shaken.*

The Book of Revelation describes much of this devastation and it is mainly described in thirds. For example:

Revelation 8:7-12 (NIV)** The first angel sounded his trumpet, and there came hail and fire mixed with blood, and it was hurled down upon the earth. A **third of the earth** was burned up, a **third of the trees** were burned up, and all the green grass was burned up. The second angel sounded his trumpet, and something like a huge mountain, all ablaze, was thrown into the sea. A **third of the sea** turned into blood, a third of the living creatures in the sea died, and a **third of the ships** were destroyed. The third angel sounded his trumpet, and a great star, blazing like a torch, fell from the sky on a **third of the rivers** and on the springs of water - the name of the star is Wormwood. A **third of the waters** turned bitter, and many people died from the waters that had become bitter. The fourth angel sounded his trumpet, and a **third of the sun** was struck, a **third of the moon**, and a **third of the stars**, so that **a third** of them turned dark. A **third of the day** was without light, and also a **third of the night [emphases added].

A further third of mankind perishes in an event described in Revelation chapter nine.

Revelation 9:18 (NIV) A third of mankind *was killed by the three plagues of fire, smoke and sulphur that came out of their mouths* [emphasis added].

This terrible devastation of the earth will occur, in my opinion, after the salvation of Israel. It is during a period that will last for at least seven years. It may correspond to that final seven year period so often discussed in eschatological circles. It will be a time of great tribulation but it will be focused over the whole earth. On the other hand, I also believe that it will be during this time that Israel begins to flourish and blossom. In fact, I believe that the entire Middle East will be a place of peace, prosperity and worship.

Isaiah 19:24-25 (RSV) *In that day Israel will be the third with Egypt and Assyria, a blessing in the midst of the earth, whom the LORD of hosts has blessed, saying, "Blessed be Egypt my people, and Assyria the work of my hands, and Israel my heritage."*

How interesting it is that Israel will be a third!

The Final Conflict

Eventually, and in the midst of the final conflict, Jesus returns to planet Earth. This was clearly stated on the Mount of Olives when Jesus ascended into Heaven.

Acts 1:11-12 (NIV) *"Men of Galilee," they said, "why do you stand here looking into the sky? This same Jesus, who has been taken from you into heaven, will come back in the same way you have seen him go into heaven." Then they returned to Jerusalem from the hill called the Mount of Olives, a Sabbath day's walk from the city.*

So he has to return to the Mount of Olives and this, in my opinion, is why East Jerusalem is the most contested geographical area on the planet at the present time. He will return in the events clearly described in Zechariah.

Zechariah 14:2-4 (NIV) *I will gather all the nations to Jerusalem to fight against it; the city will be captured, the houses ransacked, and the women raped. Half of the city will go into exile, but the rest of the people will not be taken from the city. Then the LORD will go out and fight against those nations, as he fights in the day of battle. On that day his feet will stand on the Mount of Olives, east of Jerusalem …*

These words describe a conflict which cannot be the same as that described in Zechariah chapter 12. The city of Jerusalem begins to fall (rather than remaining intact in her place) and many of the inhabitants flee through a valley that will be created by geological phenomena that have definitely not taken place yet.

There is no doubt that this final conflict will be traumatic, but to suggest that Zechariah chapter 14 is describing a holocaust, as some Bible teachers are inclined to do, is totally inappropriate.

Furthermore, if this battle is with the armies of Antichrist, as the book of Revelation seems to suggest, then one has to ask the question as to why the Antichrist needs to come to fight Jerusalem in the first place. According to some dispensational schemes, he will have already entered into a covenantal relationship with the people of Israel.

Personally, I reject all of this.

For a detailed study of the Final Battle please go to Appendix 2 (page 54).

No, this final battle will be a short lived conflict as God will intervene and the Kingdom will be totally restored to Israel simply because the King has come.[21]

In this study, I think it has become crystal clear that I, for one, believe that Israel is safe and that the modern state of Israel is a result of God's faithfulness to his promises and his commitment to bring his people back to the Land re-establishing the nation out of the ashes of the Holocaust.

Israel's Return to the Land

This national re-establishment has to be God's initiative. He who scattered Israel WILL gather them and watch over his flock like a shepherd (Jeremiah 31:10). Throughout the Tanach, the Lord is seen as the Shepherd of Israel.

Psalm 23 (RSV) *The LORD is my shepherd, I shall not want; he makes me lie down in green pastures. He leads me beside still waters; he restores my soul. He leads me in paths of righteousness for his name's sake. Even though I walk through the valley of the shadow of death, I fear no evil; for thou art with me; thy rod and thy staff, they comfort me. Thou preparest a table before me in the presence of my enemies; thou anointest my head with oil, my cup overflows. Surely goodness and mercy shall follow me all the days of my life; and I shall dwell in the house of the LORD for ever.*

Isaiah 40:10-11 (RSV) *Behold, the Lord GOD comes with might, and his arm rules for him; behold, his reward is with him, and his recompense before him. He will feed his flock like a shepherd, he will gather the lambs in his arms, he will carry them in his bosom, and gently lead those that are with young.*

---

[21] **Zechariah 14:9 (RSV)** And the LORD will become king over all the earth; on that day the LORD will be one and his name one.

Israel are Lost Sheep

Ezekiel 34:5-6 (RSV) *So they were scattered, because there was no shepherd; and they became food for all the wild beasts. My sheep were scattered, they wandered over all the mountains and on every high hill; my sheep were scattered over all the face of the earth, with none to search or seek for them.*

If salvation is both spiritual and physical to the Hebraic mind, then" lostness" must also be seen in this light. Without doubt, the analogy of the lost sheep is used as a picture of an unbeliever. Jesus used this picture.

Luke 15:4-7 (NIV) *Suppose one of you has a hundred sheep and loses one of them. Does he not leave the ninety-nine in the open country and go after the lost sheep until he finds it? And when he finds it, he joyfully puts it on his shoulders and goes home. Then he calls his friends and neighbors together and says, 'Rejoice with me; I have found my lost sheep.' I tell you that in the same way there will be more rejoicing in heaven over one sinner who repents than over ninety-nine righteous persons who do not need to repent.*

He speaks of himself as the Good Shepherd[22] which also alludes to the passage in Ezekiel.

Ezekiel 34:12 (RSV) *As a shepherd seeks out his flock when some of his sheep have been scattered abroad, so will I seek out my sheep; and I will rescue them from all places where they have been scattered on a day of clouds and thick darkness.*

---

[22] **John 10:11 (NIV)** I am the good shepherd. The good shepherd lays down his life for the sheep.

Ezekiel 34:13-16 (RSV) *And I will bring them out from the peoples, and gather them from the countries, and will bring them into their own land; and I will feed them on the mountains of Israel, by the fountains, and in all the inhabited places of the country. I will feed them with good pasture, and upon the mountain heights of Israel shall be their pasture; there they shall lie down in good grazing land, and on fat pasture they shall feed on the mountains of Israel. I myself will be the shepherd of my sheep, and I will make them lie down, says the Lord GOD. I will seek the lost, and I will bring back the strayed, and I will bind up the crippled, and I will strengthen the weak, and the fat and the strong I will watch over; I will feed them in justice.*

This is a very significant passage in our study as to whether Israel is now a safe place. The lost sheep are scattered but he goes looking for them. He leads them into their land where they will be safe. Even though they walk through the valley of the shadow of death, the rod and staff of the Good Shepherd leads them on. If this is not true of modern Israel, then there has to be another scattering of the flock. This is taught by some Messianic teachers but there is no mention of it in Scripture. In fact, there are only two re-gatherings mentioned.

Isaiah 11:10-12 (RSV) *In that day the root of Jesse shall stand as an ensign to the peoples; him shall the nations seek, and his dwellings shall be glorious. In that day the Lord will extend his hand yet a second time to recover the remnant which is left of his people, from Assyria, from Egypt, from Pathros, from Ethiopia, from Elam, from Shinar, from Hamath, and from the coastlands of the sea. He will raise an ensign for the nations, and will assemble the outcasts of Israel, and gather the dispersed of Judah from the four corners of the earth.*

The Root of Jesse is the Messiah, the Son of David. Something has happened between the first and second re-gatherings that has taken the knowledge of the Messiah to all the Nations since they are now in a position to rally to him.[23] If the first re-gathering was only out of Babylon (and maybe Assyria); then the second re-gathering is from the four quarters of the earth.

This HAS to be the situation today. The point is this; there is no mention of a third re-gathering which presumably would need to be the case if modern Israel was just a political anomaly. This second re-gathering is seen as a banner in the Nations. God's faithfulness is on display in the return to the Land. It may be controversial for many but that is actually the point. It is his honor that is at stake.

Ezekiel 36:22-24 (RSV) *Therefore say to the house of Israel, Thus says the Lord GOD: It is not for your sake, O house of Israel, that I am about to act, but for the sake of my holy name, which you have profaned among the nations to which you came. And I will vindicate the holiness of my great name, which has been profaned among the nations, and which you have profaned among them; and the nations will know that I am the LORD, says the Lord GOD, when through you I vindicate my holiness before their eyes. For I will take you from the nations, and gather you from all the countries, and bring you into your own land.*

---

[23] During this rallying of the Nations, the resting place of the Messiah is a glorious one but that is another subject.

The Good Shepherd [24]

---

[24] The Good Shepherd by Alfred Soord (1868-1915) .

Israel Returns to the Land Out of Holocaust

As we have seen repeatedly, the Bible makes very clear that towards the end of this age; God will take the initiative and bring his people back to the Land. This is recorded in both the Old and the New Testaments. In many of these prophetic passages, God brings his people back out of a holocaust. Here are some further examples.

Isaiah 42:23-25 (NIV) *Which of you will listen to this or pay close attention in time to come? Who handed Jacob over to become loot and Israel to the plunderers? Was it not the LORD, against whom we have sinned? For they would not follow his ways; they did not obey his law. So he poured out on them his burning anger, the violence of war. It enveloped them in flames, yet they did not understand; it consumed them, but they did not take it to heart.*

If ever there was a passage that described **the** Holocaust, it is this passage. The implications of what is being said here are enormous and are, perhaps, beyond the scope of this essay. However, it is important to realize that the chapters and verses into which the modern Bible is divided are a *relatively* modern innovation and not inspired. In fact, many times, this division inhibits a clearer understanding of what the passage is trying to say. Let us continue it into the next chapter.

Isaiah 43:1-3 (NIV) *But now, this is what the LORD says, he who created you, O Jacob, he who formed you, O Israel: "Fear not, for I have redeemed you; I have summoned you by name; you are mine. When you pass through the waters, I will be with you; and when you pass through the rivers, they will not sweep over you. When you walk through the fire, you will not be burned; the flames will not set you ablaze. For I am the LORD, your God, the Holy One of Israel, your Savior; I give Egypt for your ransom, Cush and Seba in your stead ...*

***Isaiah 43:4-7 (NIV)** Since you are precious and honored in my sight, and because I love you, I will give men in exchange for you, and people in exchange for your life. Do not be afraid, for I am with you; I will bring your children from the east and gather you from the west. I will say to the north, 'Give them up!' and to the south, 'Do not hold them back.' Bring my sons from afar and my daughters from the ends of the earth - everyone who is called by my name, whom I created for my glory, whom I formed and made."*

Very often, Christians only consider the first verses of Isaiah chapter 43. In fact, they often find their way into "promise boxes" and Christian homilies. However the words of chapter 43 begin, in nearly all English translations, with the words "But now". It is possibly slightly more accurate to say "And now". Whatever the best translation might be, without question, the beginning of Isaiah chapter 43 follows on from the end of chapter 42. In other words, God brings his sons and daughters back from the four quarters of the earth out of holocaust.

Returning out of Holocaust

Jeremiah 30:1-7 (NIV) *This is the word that came to Jeremiah from the LORD: "This is what the LORD, the God of Israel, says: 'Write in a book all the words I have spoken to you. The days are coming,' declares the LORD, 'when I will bring my people Israel and Judah back from captivity and restore them to the land I gave their forefathers to possess,' says the LORD." These are the words the LORD spoke concerning Israel and Judah: "This is what the LORD says: "'Cries of fear are heard - terror, not peace. Ask and see: Can a man bear children? Then why do I see every strong man with his hands on his stomach like a woman in labor, every face turned deathly pale? How awful that day will be! None will be like it. It will be a time of trouble for Jacob, but he will be saved out of it.*

Chapters 30 and 31 of the prophecy of Jeremiah are the most important in our study. In fact, an entire book could be written entitled *"The Time of Jacob's Trouble"*. Perhaps this author will develop this present essay to encompass this in due course. Without doubt, the actual meaning of "the time of Jacob's trouble" is critical in our understanding of whether Israel is safe or not. Put simply, if *"the time of Jacob's trouble"* is still future and is to be equated with *"the Great Tribulation"*, Israel is definitely not safe now. However, the question would then have to be asked, namely, why would God bring his people back to the land if the worst is still to come? Such a thought is totally contrary to everything we have come to understand about the character of the God of Israel. After all,

Exodus 3:15 (NIV) *God also said to Moses, "Say to the Israelites, 'The LORD, the God of your fathers - the God of Abraham, the God of Isaac and the God of Jacob - has sent me to you.'* **This is my name forever, the name by which I am to be remembered from generation to generation** [emphasis added].

However, this author believes that chapters 30 and 31 of Jeremiah describe a prophetic chronology. The chapters begin with a prologue and overview (Jeremiah 30:1-3). God reveals to Jeremiah his ultimate purposes. He will bring Israel and Judah back to the land of their forefathers. We need to note that this word (and, for that matter, subsequent promises in these chapters) is made both to Israel <u>and</u> Judah. Why should this be so? It is an historical fact, that in the days of Jeremiah, the Davidic Kingdom of Israel had become divided into two parts.

The northern kingdom was known as Israel (or Ephraim) and comprised approximately 10 tribes, subjugated and taken into captivity during the Assyrian invasion in the 8th century BC; the southern Kingdom was known as Judah and consisted predominately of the tribes of Judah and Benjamin with some additions from the tribes of Simeon and Levi. The future return to the Land, however, encompasses all 12 tribes. In other words, there are no 10 lost tribes to the Lord. He who scattered Israel (i.e.12 tribes) will gather them. Again the significance of these words is somewhat beyond the scope of this essay. However, whatever these words actually mean, at the re-gathering (or perhaps sometime afterwards) there will also be a re-unification. For example,

Ezekiel 37:21-22 (RSV) *Thus says the Lord GOD: Behold, I will take the people of Israel from the nations among which they have gone, and will gather them from all sides, and bring them to their own land; and I will make them one nation in the land, upon the mountains of Israel; and one king shall be king over them all; and they shall be no longer two nations, and no longer divided into two kingdoms.*

In other words, there is no two-state solution, only one! But, more significantly, these words in Jeremiah chapter 30 **cannot** refer to the return from Babylon which involved just the southern Kingdom of Judah which had been taken into captivity in the 6th century BCE with only a remnant returning after 70 years. The words in Jeremiah 30 look into the distant future at a second re-gathering that we have already considered as described in the prophecy of Isaiah.

Isaiah 11:11-14 (NIV) *In that day the Lord will reach out his hand **a second time** to reclaim the remnant that is left of his people **from Assyria**, from Lower Egypt, from Upper Egypt, from Cush, from Elam, from Babylonia, from Hamath and from the islands of the sea. He will raise a banner for the nations and **gather the exiles of Israel; he will assemble the scattered people of Judah from the four quarters of the earth. Ephraim's jealousy will vanish, and Judah's enemies will be cut off; Ephraim will not be jealous of Judah, nor Judah hostile towards Ephraim.** They will swoop down on the slopes of Philistia to the west; together they will plunder the people to the east. They will lay hands on Edom and Moab, and the Ammonites will be subject to them* [emphases added].

This second re-gathering is far greater than that which took place at the return from Babylon. It is also interesting to note that the schism, jealousy and hostility between Judah and Ephraim will disappear. The significance of these words is profound but again beyond the scope of this essay.

It is this author's opinion that the second section in these chapters in Jeremiah describes the Shoah. Let's look at them again.

Jeremiah 30:4-7 (NIV) *These are the words the LORD spoke concerning Israel and Judah: "This is what the LORD says: "'Cries of fear are heard - terror, not peace. Ask and see: Can a man bear children? Then why do I see every strong man with his hands on his stomach like a woman in labor, every face turned deathly pale? How awful that day will be! None will be like it. It will be a time of trouble for Jacob, but he will be saved out of it.*

Every Face turned Deathly Pale

The reason this author is convinced that these verses refer primarily to the Holocaust which took place in the Second World War is what subsequently is described by the next verses in Jeremiah chapter 30.

Jeremiah 30:8-10 (RSV) *And it shall come to pass in that day, says the LORD of hosts, that I will break the yoke from off their neck, and I will burst their bonds, and strangers shall no more make servants of them. But they shall serve the LORD their God and David their king, whom I will raise up for them. Then fear not, O Jacob my servant, says the LORD, nor be dismayed, O Israel; for lo, I will save you from afar, and your offspring from the land of their captivity. Jacob shall return and have quiet and ease, and none shall make him afraid.*

These verses are also a prophetic overview and events that probably encompass many years are condensed into three short verses. Here we see again that salvation for the people of Israel (and perhaps for everyone for that matter) has a physical as well as a spiritual dimension. The physical dimension is expressed in the fact that no longer will foreigners enslave them; that their long exile will end from the distant places where they had been scattered.

Furthermore, Jacob (i.e. Israel) will have peace and security and no-one will make them afraid. In spite of enormous global and regional opposition, I suggest that this describes modern Israel rather well as they stand today in their own strength (see also Ezekiel 39:26). However, in addition to these physical realities, Israel will ultimately know spiritual revival and they will serve the Lord their God. In other words, all Israel will be saved.

Jeremiah 30:11 (RSV) For I am with you to save you, *says the LORD; I will make a full end of all the nations among whom I scattered you, but of you I will not make a full end. I will chasten you in just measure, and I will by no means leave you unpunished* [emphasis added].

These words perfectly echo Isaiah chapters 42 and 43. The following verses in Jeremiah chapter 30 describe the open wound and the subsequent supernatural healing of Israel.

Jeremiah 30:12-15 (RSV) *For thus says the LORD: Your hurt is incurable, and your wound is grievous. There is none to uphold your cause, no medicine for your wound, no healing for you. All your lovers have forgotten you; they care nothing for you; for I have dealt you the blow of an enemy, the punishment of a merciless foe, because your guilt is great, because your sins are flagrant. Why do you cry out over your hurt? Your pain is incurable. Because your guilt is great, because your sins are flagrant, I have done these things to you.*

If "the time of Jacob's trouble" was the Holocaust, it is possible to conclude that this tragedy continues to be **the** open wound that requires healing. It also leads us to the theological necessity of appreciating that, at the very least, God allowed the Holocaust. However, he continues to be a God of grace.

***Jeremiah 30:16-17 (RSV)** Therefore all who devour you shall be devoured, and all your foes, every one of them, shall go into captivity; those who despoil you shall become a spoil, and all who prey on you I will make a prey. For I will restore health to you, and your wounds I will heal, says the LORD, because they have called you an outcast: It is Zion, for whom no one cares!*

God is withdrawing all foreign support from Israel at this time. Anti-Semitism has made its way for anti-Zionism. It has to be so because God is going to do something quite remarkable in the days to come. He is going to reveal the holiness of his great name in the sight of many nations (Ezekiel 39:27). In addition, the open wound of the people of Israel will be healed by him.

***Isaiah 61:1-3 (NIV)** The Spirit of the Sovereign LORD is on me … to proclaim … the day of vengeance of our God, to comfort all who mourn, and provide for those who grieve in Zion - to bestow on them a crown of beauty instead of ashes, the oil of gladness instead of mourning, and a garment of praise instead of a spirit of despair.*

Jesus did not read these words in the synagogue in Nazareth (Luke 4:18-19). The time was not right then. I believe that we will live to see the fulfillment of these words.

Jeremiah 30:18-22 describes the re-establishment of the nation, its government and population increase. All this has happened since the Holocaust. The final verses in Jeremiah chapter 30 again summarize the purposes of God.

Jeremiah 30:23-24 (RSV) *Behold the storm of the LORD! Wrath has gone forth, a whirling tempest; it will burst upon the head of the wicked. The fierce anger of the LORD will not turn back until he has executed and accomplished the intents of his mind. In the latter days you will understand this.*

Jeremiah chapter 31 begins in the same vein.

Jeremiah 31:1-2 (NIV) *"At that time," declares the LORD, "I will be the God of all the clans of Israel, and they will be my people." This is what the LORD says: "The people who survive the sword will find favor in the desert; I will come to give rest to Israel."*

Obviously the *"at that time"* refers to the *"latter days"* described at the end of chapter 30. The people who survived the sword found favor in the desert. Only a remnant has returned to the Land but here they find rest. Prior to Aliyah which began in modern times in the late 19th century, Israel was a desolate waste. We are reminded of the words of Mark Twain who visited Palestine in 1867.

> " *...[a] desolate country whose soil is rich enough, but is given over wholly to weeds-a silent mournful expanse....A desolation is here that not even imagination can grace with the pomp of life and action....We never saw a human being on the whole route....There was hardly a tree or a shrub anywhere. Even the olive and the cactus, those fast friends of the worthless soil, had almost deserted the country.* " [25]

---

[25] Mark Twain, The Innocents Abroad. London: 1881 (New American Library, 1997).

Although this historical perspective has been challenged by some Palestinian historians,[26] the restoration of Israel's homeland was largely undertaken by Jewish pioneers. Prior to this, the land of Israel had become a desert.

Through hard labor and the loss of many lives, the remnant who had survived the sword found favor in the desert.

Jewish Pioneers, 1921

The next verses in Jeremiah 31, further describe the reclamation of the land and national life. Among these verses, the following are very significant because they are an exhortation to the nations of the world to recognize what God is doing.

Jeremiah 31:7 (NIV) *This is what the LORD says: "Sing with joy for Jacob; shout for the foremost of the nations. Make your praises heard, and say, 'O LORD, save your people, the remnant of Israel.'*

---

[26] http://www.palestineremembered.com/Acre/Articles/Story845.html

So how does God indicate that he has heard the prayers of believers in the nations? The next verse tells us how.

Jeremiah 31:8 (NIV) *See, I will bring them from the land of the north and gather them from the ends of the earth. Among them will be the blind and the lame, expectant mothers and women in labor; a great throng will return.*

Thus, it is totally consistent to see that the salvation of Israel has a physical as well as a spiritual dimension. This verse accurately describes the increase in Aliyah that took place after the establishment of the nation in 1948. Almost by definition, they must return in unbelief because it is in the land that God will reveal himself to the nation. We shall return to this theme shortly.

If *"the time of Jacob's trouble"* is still future, one has to conclude that the re-establishment of Israel is simply a political accident. Furthermore, the current state of Israel has to be totally dismantled, the people sent again into exile and the land returned to its desert state. This is a totally illogical conclusion to make although several Messianic teachers are inclined to do so.

Jeremiah 31:15 (NIV) *This is what the LORD says: "A voice is heard in Ramah, mourning and great weeping, Rachel weeping for her children and refusing to be comforted, because her children are no more."*

Again Jeremiah 31:15 is a prophetic motif that has repeated throughout history. The words were fulfilled at the Babylonian exile, at the time of Herod, and throughout Jewish history. However, the time has come for verses 16 and 17 to be fulfilled in their entirety.

Jeremiah 31:16-17 (RSV) *Thus says the LORD: "Keep your voice from weeping, and your eyes from tears; for your work shall be rewarded, says the LORD, and they shall come back from the land of the enemy. There is hope for your future, says the LORD, and your children shall come back to their own country.*

The return to the land out of holocaust is prerequisite for all that the Lord is going to do in the land and in the lives all those that have returned.

Jeremiah 31:27-28 (NIV) *"The days are coming," declares the LORD, "when I will plant the house of Israel and the house of Judah with the offspring of men and of animals. Just as I watched over them to uproot and tear down, and to overthrow, destroy and bring disaster, so I will watch over them to build and to plant," declares the LORD."*

The remaining verses of Jeremiah chapter 31 describe the establishment of the new covenant which again is a prophetic motif that was initially fulfilled on the day of Pentecost. However, again we wait for the day when it will be truly said:

Jeremiah 31:34 (NIV) *No longer will a man teach his neighbor, or a man his brother, saying, 'Know the LORD,' because they will all know me, from the least of them to the greatest," declares the LORD. "For I will forgive their wickedness and will remember their sins no more."*

The Valley of the Dry Bones

Another passage that graphically describes the return of the people of Israel to the land out of holocaust is the famous passage in Ezekiel where the prophet had a vision of a valley filled with bones.

Ezekiel 37:1-3 (RSV) *The hand of the LORD was upon me, and he brought me out by the Spirit of the LORD, and set me down in the midst of the valley; it was full of bones. And he led me round among them; and behold, there were very many upon the valley; and lo, they were very dry and he said to me, "Son of man, can these bones live?" And I answered, "O Lord GOD, thou knowest."*

Bergen Belsen

Personally, I am convinced that the prophet Ezekiel had a glimpse of the horror of **the** Holocaust. It could have been the mass graves at Bergen Belsen or maybe the valley that was Babi Yar on the outskirts of Kiev where, on September 29–30 1941, 33,771 Jews were killed in a single operation.

Babi Yar Ravine on the Outskirts of Kiev, Ukraine

Whatever Ezekiel saw, he also heard the words of the Lord.

Ezekiel 37:11-14 (RSV) *Then he said to me, "Son of man, these bones are the whole house of Israel. Behold, they say, 'Our bones are dried up, and our hope is lost; we are clean cut off.' Therefore prophesy, and say to them, Thus says the Lord GOD: Behold, I will open your graves, and raise you from your graves, O my people; and I will bring you home into the land of Israel. And you shall know that I am the LORD, when I open your graves, and raise you from your graves, O my people. And I will put my Spirit within you, and you shall live, and I will place you in your own land; then you shall know that I, the LORD, have spoken, and I have done it, says the LORD."*

It is not too complicated to understand. Out of the ashes of the Holocaust, God promises to bring his people back to the land of Israel. Once back in the land, a spiritual revival will take place. Accordingly, Israel returns to the land in unbelief. This is understandable, for many Jewish people the very fact of the Holocaust has undermined any belief in a loving God.

Israel Returns to the Land in Unbelief

God takes a people that have profaned his name out of the nations where they were scattered. Once they are back in the Land, God takes further initiative.

Ezekiel 36:24-28 (RSV) *For I will take you from the nations, and gather you from all the countries, and bring you into your own land. I will sprinkle clean water upon you, and you shall be clean from all your uncleanness, and from all your idols I will cleanse you. A new heart I will give you, and a new spirit I will put within you; and I will take out of your flesh the heart of stone and give you a heart of flesh. And I will put my spirit within you, and cause you to walk in my statutes and be careful to observe my ordinances. You shall dwell in the land which I gave to your fathers; and you shall be my people, and I will be your God.*

If it is suggested that the modern state of Israel has a heart of stone and is destined for judgment, so what? This is to be expected according to the order of events prophesied in scripture. We are waiting for God's initiative to give them a new heart and a new spirit.

Isaiah 42:16 (RSV) *I will lead the blind in a way that they know not, in paths that they have not known I will guide them. I will turn the darkness before them into light, the rough places into level ground. These are the things I will do, and I will not forsake them.*

If Israel is not Safe,
We can be Certain of Nothing

This to me is the bottom line. If Israel is not safe, everything is uncertain. There are no guarantees of anything except that God is God and our ultimate destiny is unknown. But let us, for the sake of argument, accept that God's promises as expressed in the Bible are straightforward and relevant for our day. If this is the case then the re-establishment of Israel is the clearest demonstration of his faithfulness. Yes, the nation has been re-gathered in unbelief but we are awaiting the most momentous event in the recent history of mankind.

Is Israel the only Safe Place
for the Jewish people?

I think that the answer has to be yes. We can be confident that God will watch over his re-gathered flock. This seems to be the testimony of Israel since its re-establishment in 1948. They survived, inexplicably, the war of Independence and came through numerous other conflicts, largely unscathed although many soldiers have been lost in battle.

However, the situation is deteriorating politically as the surrounding nations are gearing up for what they perceive to be the final battle and the eradication of the Zionist regime.[27] Again this should come as no surprise as scripture clearly indicates that this would be the case. The following psalm seems to be relevant to the current situation.

---

[27] This is setting the scene for Zechariah 12 to be fulfilled

***Psalm 83 (NIV)** O God, do not keep silent; be not quiet, O God, be not still. See how your enemies are astir, how your foes rear their heads. With cunning they conspire against your people; they plot against those you cherish. "Come," they say, "let us destroy them as a nation, that the name of Israel be remembered no more." With one mind they plot together; they form an alliance against you … Let them know that you, whose name is the LORD, that you alone are the Most High over all the earth.*

Salvation is both physical and spiritual. Israel's survival (i.e. their safety) is the phenomenon that will convince the world that God is who he says he is.

***Ezekiel 39:7-8 (RSV)** And my holy name I will make known in the midst of my people Israel; and I will not let my holy name be profaned any more; and the nations shall know that I am the LORD, the Holy One in Israel. Behold, it is coming and it will be brought about, says the Lord GOD. That is the day of which I have spoken.*

Personally, I cannot wait for this to take place. I am sure that the days leading up to this event will be filled with gloom, desperation and despondency. All will appear completely hopeless. Humanly speaking Israel will seem to be finished. They will face insuperable odds. Probably, a lot of people will be fleeing the country. Embassies will be withdrawing their staff. Christian organizations will suggest that their people leave. Our family will be pleading for us to get out. This is the perfect scenario for God to intervene.[28]

---

[28] I believe that the story of Joseph may be repeated in the days to come, namely, **Genesis 45:1 (NIV)** So there was no-one with Joseph when he made himself known to his brothers.

__Psalm 2:1-6 (NIV)__ Why do the nations conspire and the peoples plot in vain? The kings of the earth take their stand and the rulers gather together against the LORD and against his Anointed One. "Let us break their chains," they say, "and throw off their fetters." The One enthroned in heaven laughs; the Lord scoffs at them. Then he rebukes them in his anger and terrifies them in his wrath, saying, "I have installed my King on Zion, my holy hill."

__Isaiah 60:1-2 (RSV)__ Arise, shine; for your light has come, and the glory of the LORD has risen upon you. For behold, darkness shall cover the earth, and thick darkness the peoples; but the LORD will arise upon you, and his glory will be seen upon you.

Is Anywhere Else Safe?

I am not sure. In this great conflict, we read these verses.

__Ezekiel 39:4-8 (NIV)__ On the mountains of Israel you will fall, you and all your troops and the nations with you. I will give you as food to all kinds of carrion birds and to the wild animals. You will fall in the open field, for I have spoken, declares the Sovereign LORD. __I will send fire on Magog and on those who live in safety in the coastlands, and they will know that I am the LORD.__ "'I will make known my holy name among my people Israel. I will no longer let my holy name be profaned, and the nations will know that I the LORD am the Holy One in Israel. It is coming! It will surely take place, declares the Sovereign LORD. This is the day I have spoken of [emphasis added].

Magog (i.e. from Gog) is the collective places from where the invading armies that will attack Israel have come. These places will not be safe. But there is another ill-defined area called "the coastlands" which will experience fire on that day. Where and what are the coastlands? These are distant places that are bordered by sea.

Jeremiah 31:10-11 (NIV) *Hear the word of the LORD, O nations; proclaim it in distant coastlands: 'He who scattered Israel will gather them and will watch over his flock like a shepherd.' For the LORD will ransom Jacob and redeem them from the hand of those stronger than they.*

One can see the sense in proclaiming this truth in the prophecy of Jeremiah in the distant coastlands. People need to be prepared for what God is going to do in the world. At the time of the conflict in the Middle East, the coastlands will appear to live in safety but it will not last. Personally, I believe that this describes the Western World. God holds the nations accountable for their actions towards the people of Abraham.

Genesis 12:2-3 (RSV) *And I will make of you a great nation, and I will bless you, and make your name great, so that you will be a blessing. I will bless those who bless you, and him who curses you I will curse; and by you all the families of the earth shall bless themselves.*

Isaiah 60:12 (NIV) *For the nation or kingdom that will not serve you will perish; it will be utterly ruined.*

No nation on earth tried harder to block the re-establishment of Israel more than Great Britain. In 1948, Great Britain had an empire that spanned the globe. Today it has virtually nothing. The USA has followed Britain in its responsibility to oversee the well-being of Israel and it is turning its back on this responsibility. The coastlands of America are situated on geological fault lines that are only held in check by God's mercy.

So will Anywhere be Safe?

God declares that he will devastate the earth before the end of this age (e.g. Isaiah 24). He also states categorically:

Jeremiah 30:11 (NIV) I am with you and will save you,' declares the LORD. 'Though I completely destroy all the nations among which I scatter you, I will not completely destroy you. I will discipline you but only with justice; I will not let you go entirely unpunished.'

Quite what the complete destruction of the nations into which the Jewish people were scattered means, only time will tell. But it has to mean that these nations are not safe. However, I do believe that there will be cities of refuge for believers to flee to. This was definitely true for the Israelites in Egypt.

Exodus 8:22-23 (NIV) On that day I will deal differently with the land of Goshen, where my people live … so that you will know that I, the LORD, am in this land. I will make a distinction between my people and your people.

I believe this distinction will be made in the days to come but it might be important to identify those places which will be safe. However, more than anything else, our ultimate place of safety is in God himself.

Psalm 27:3-5 (NIV) Though an army besiege me, my heart will not fear; though war break out against me, even then will I be confident. One thing I ask of the LORD, this is what I seek: that I may dwell in the house of the LORD all the days of my life, to gaze upon the beauty of the LORD and to seek him in his temple. For in the day of trouble he will keep me safe in his dwelling; he will hide me in the shelter of his tabernacle and set me high upon a rock.

***Psalm 91 (RSV)** He who dwells in the shelter of the Most High, who abides in the shadow of the Almighty, will say to the LORD, "My refuge and my fortress; my God, in whom I trust."*

For he will deliver you from the snare of the fowler and from the deadly pestilence; he will cover you with his pinions, and under his wings you will find refuge; his faithfulness is a shield and buckler.

You will not fear the terror of the night, nor the arrow that flies by day, nor the pestilence that stalks in darkness, nor the destruction that wastes at noonday. A thousand may fall at your side, ten thousand at your right hand; but it will not come near you. You will only look with your eyes and see the recompense of the wicked.

Because you have made the LORD your refuge, the Most High your habitation, no evil shall befall you, no scourge come near your tent. For he will give his angels charge of you to guard you in all your ways. On their hands they will bear you up, lest you dash your foot against a stone.

You will tread on the lion and the adder, the young lion and the serpent you will trample under foot.

Because he cleaves to me in love, I will deliver him; I will protect him, because he knows my name. When he calls to me, I will answer him; I will be with him in trouble, I will rescue him and honor him. With long life I will satisfy him, and show him my salvation.

Appendix 1: Holocaust

The word "Holocaust" is very ancient. It is derived from the Greek *holókaustós* [ὀλόκαυστος] and literally means: hólos, "whole" and kaustós, "burnt". It was used in pagan Greek ritual and described an offering that was totally consumed by fire.

The Septuagint (the Greek translation of the Hebrew Bible), completed in the 2nd century BCE, consistently translated the Hebrew word olah [עוֹלָה] with a derivative of the Greek word *holókaustós*, namely, *holokautōma* [ὀλοκαύτωμα]. The Hebrew word olah literally means *"that which is offered up"*; it signifies a burnt offering offered whole to the Lord.

An interesting example is in Psalm 40:6

Psalm 40:6 (KJV) *Sacrifice and offering thou didst not desire; mine ears hast thou opened:* **burnt offering** *and sin offering hast thou not required.*

Psalm 39:7 (Septuagint equivalent verse) θυσίαν καὶ προσφορὰν οὐκ ἠθέλησας ὠτία δὲ κατηρτίσω μοι ὀλοκαύτωμα καὶ περὶ ἁμαρτίας οὐκ ἤτησας

The word also appears in Latin as *holocaustum* and was used in the Middle Ages to describe animal sacrifices in the Bible.

For example, Numbers 28:19 in the Latin Vulgate:

> offeretisque incensum **holocaustum** Domino
> vitulos de armento duos arietem unum agnos
> anniculos inmaculatos septem

This verse in the NIV is translated: *But you shall offer an offering made by fire, a burnt offering to the Lord: two young bulls, one ram, and seven male lambs a year old; they shall be without blemish to the best of your knowledge.*

Throughout history, the word has been used in the general sense for great destruction resulting in the extensive loss of life, especially by fire. It is important to note, however, that the word became connected to the murder of the six million in more recent times. It is only from the 1960's that the word was used by scholars and popular writers to specifically refer to the Nazi Genocide. Remarkably, it was the television mini-series (1978) which was entitled *"Holocaust"* that brought this word and its association with the Jewish people into more common usage.

The biblical word "Shoah" [שׁוֹאָה] meaning calamity, desolation or destruction, is the preferred word in Israel to describe the Nazi genocide during the Second World War. Perhaps it is preferred mainly because of the ancient pagan association of the word *holocaust*. Perhaps there are other reasons.

The word Shoah appears in Psalm 35:8

Psalm 35:8 (KJV) *Let destruction [שׁוֹאָה] come upon him at unawares; and let his net that he hath hid catch himself: into that very destruction [בְּשׁוֹאָה literally "into destruction"].*

Also and very significantly,

Isaiah 47:11 (KJV) *Therefore shall evil come upon thee; thou shalt not know from whence it riseth: and mischief shall fall upon thee; thou shalt not be able to put it off: and desolation [שׁוֹאָה] shall come upon thee suddenly, which thou shalt not know.*

Appendix 2: The Final Battle

One of the significant concerns that is raised in response to any suggestion that Israel is now the only safe place for Jewish people is the biblical detail of the final battle which obviously takes place in Jerusalem. In particular, Zechariah states unequivocally:

Zechariah 14:2 (NKJV) *For I will gather all the nations to battle against Jerusalem; the city shall be taken, the houses rifled, and the women ravished. Half of the city shall go into captivity, but the remnant of the people shall not be cut off from the city.*

There is no doubting that this will be a very traumatic period. At least half of the city will be captured, the houses ransacked and women are raped. There is no denying this. But even here, the Lord makes a way to bring his people to a safe place.

Zechariah 14:3-5 (NKJV) *Then the LORD will go forth and fight against those nations as He fights in the day of battle. And in that day His feet will stand on the Mount of Olives which faces Jerusalem on the east and the Mount of Olives shall be split in two from east to west making a very large valley; half of the mountain shall move toward the north and half of it toward the south. Then you shall flee through my mountain valley.*

As we will see, his feet standing on the Mount of Olives, triggers an earthquake that creates a wide valley through the Mount of Olives. It is through this valley that at least half of the population of Jerusalem will be able to flee to safety.

I believe that this climactic event will also parallel one that took place during the Exodus.

***Exodus 14:21-22 (RSV)** Then Moses stretched out his hand over the sea; and the LORD drove the sea back by a strong east wind all night, and made the sea dry land, and the waters were divided. And the people of Israel went into the midst of the sea on dry ground, the waters being a wall to them on their right hand and on their left.*

At the last, it will not be the sea that is divided, but the Mount of Olives. A level path will be created that will bring his people to safety and away from the advancing armies. It is worth dwelling on the Exodus story a little longer. The armies of Egypt were closing in on the Israelites and the people were afraid. In response, Moses encourages his people:

***Exodus 14:13-14 (RSV)** And Moses said to the people, "Fear not, stand firm, and see the salvation of the LORD, which he will work for you today; for the Egyptians whom you see today, you shall never see again. The LORD will fight for you, and you have only to be still."*

I believe the situation at the last will be the same. As the armies advance toward Jerusalem, the western suburbs of the city will begin to move eastwards. They will know the scriptures and they will be encouraged to flee to safety to the Mount of Olives. With their backs up against a wall, they will begin to look up and they will once more cry "hosanna".

***Psalm 118:25-26 (NIV)** O LORD, save us; O LORD, grant us success. Blessed is he who comes in the name of the LORD.*

For Jesus also said to Jerusalem.

***Matthew 23:39 (NIV)** For I tell you, you will not see me again until you say, 'Blessed is he who comes in the name of the Lord.'"*

This cry of hosanna (save us now) is the signal for Jesus to return to Jerusalem. This is further indication that the nation will have come to faith prior to this event. In addition, Jesus knows that a day would come when Psalm 118 would be fulfilled in its entirety. For example,

Psalm 118:10-14 (RSV) *All nations surrounded me; in the name of the LORD I cut them off! They surrounded me, surrounded me on every side; in the name of the LORD I cut them off! They surrounded me like bees, they blazed like a fire of thorns; in the name of the LORD I cut them off! I was pushed hard, so that I was falling, but the LORD helped me.* **The LORD is my strength and my song; he has become my salvation** [emphasis added].

It is worth noting that the name of the Lord is mentioned three times in this passage and it is Jesus who has been given the name that is above every name.[29]

This is such an important passage and a very significant refrain, namely "the LORD is my strength and my song; he has become my salvation". It is worth noting other scriptures where this specific refrain is also mentioned. Without doubt, the most significant is the song of Moses.

Exodus 15:1-2 (RSV) *Then Moses and the people of Israel sang this song to the LORD, saying, "I will sing to the LORD, for he has triumphed gloriously; the horse and his rider he has thrown into the sea.* **The LORD is my strength and my song, and he has become my salvation** [emphasis added].

---

[29] **Philippians 2:9-11 (RSV)** Therefore God has highly exalted him and bestowed on him the name which is above every name, that at the name of Jesus every knee should bow, in heaven and on earth and under the earth, and every tongue confess that Jesus Christ is Lord, to the glory of God the Father.

Thus, the song of Moses links the Exodus miracle with the final battle. It is no wonder that we read this in the book of Revelation.

Revelation 15:1-3 (RSV) *Then I saw another portent in heaven, great and wonderful, seven angels with seven plagues, which are the last, for with them the wrath of God is ended. And I saw what appeared to be a sea of glass mingled with fire, and those who had conquered the beast and its image and the number of its name, standing beside the sea of glass with harps of God in their hands.* ***And they sing the song of Moses, the servant of God, <u>and</u> the song of the Lamb*** [emphasis added].

So the final battle will obviously be traumatic but it will certainly not be another holocaust as some Bible teachers would suggest.[30] It is also appropriate to consider what the New Testament adds to the detail of the final battle.

Revelation 16:12-16 (RSV) *The sixth angel poured his bowl on the great river Euphrates, and its water was dried up, to prepare the way for the kings from the east. And I saw, issuing from the mouth of the dragon and from the mouth of the beast and from the mouth of the false prophet, three foul spirits like frogs; for they are demonic spirits, performing signs, who go abroad to the kings of the whole world, to assemble them for battle on the great day of God the Almighty. "Lo, I am coming like a thief! Blessed is he who is awake, keeping his garments that he may not go naked and be seen exposed!" And they assembled them at the place which is called in Hebrew Armageddon.*

---

[30] For example, J. David Pawson http://davidpawson.org/resources/ resource/1316?return_url=http%3A%2F%2Fdavidpawson.org%2Fresources% 2Fcategory%2Fold-testament-studies%2Fzechariah%2F

Although it is known as the battle of Armageddon, as we have seen, the final battle will take place in Jerusalem. It particularly involves the "kings of the east" but also the "kings of the whole world". This is consistent with the event as described in Zechariah chapter 14. The build up to this final trauma obviously takes time. The river Euphrates is dried up to allow the "kings of the east" free passage. This is alluded to earlier in the book of Revelation.

Revelation 9:14-16 (NIV) *It said to the sixth angel who had the trumpet, "Release the four angels who are bound at the great river Euphrates." And the four angels who had been kept ready for this very hour and day and month and year were released to kill a third of mankind. The number of the mounted troops was two hundred million. I heard their number.*

The only nation that could boast this number of troops is the nation of China. At the last, it may be that this nation has become the world's major (and perhaps only) superpower. I get the impression that this is a new crusade to liberate the city of Jerusalem. As the "kings of the east" are making their way to Israel, all the other nations are also coming to "face them".

Israel and China

It is worth noting the strong relationship that is being established between Israel and China. For example, the two countries have now signed an accord which allows citizens of both countries to have ten year visas to visit each other.[31]

---

[31] The deal will allow Israeli businesspeople and tourists to enter China multiple times with the same visa, which will be valid for a decade. The same will apply for Chinese citizens visiting Israel, an arrangement which Jerusalem hopes will help increase tourism [taken from http://www.timesofisrael.com/israel-and-china-to-sign-10-year-multiple-entry-visa-deal]

It is also very interesting to realize that the nation of China is specifically mentioned in the Tanach.

Isaiah 49:12 (KJV) *Behold, these shall come from far: and, lo, these from the north and from the west; and these **from the land of Sinim*** [emphasis added].

Although the word has been interpreted differently in English translations of the Bible, the "Sinim" [סינים] are the Chinese in the Hebrew language. Historically, there has been a Jewish presence in China for millennia.[32] Many have returned and are returning to Israel.[33] It is also significant that the church in China is growing at a phenomenal rate.[34] Moreover, the main Christian support for the nation of Israel is now coming from the nations in the East rather than the West. Perhaps this was also prophesied in Scripture.

Isaiah 46:11-13 (NIV) *From the east I summon a bird of prey; **from a far-off land, a man to fulfill my purpose**. What I have said, that will I bring about; what I have planned, that will I do. Listen to me, you stubborn-hearted, you who are far from righteousness. I am bringing my righteousness near, it is not far away; and my salvation will not be delayed. I will grant salvation to Zion, my splendor to Israel* [emphasis added].

On their march to Jerusalem, this vast army of the "kings of the east" also becomes the instrument of global judgment in the hands of the four angels. One-third of mankind will be killed at this time (Revelation 9:18).

---

[32] http://www.jewsofchina.org/

[33] http://forward.com/news/334261/making-aliyah-chinese-jews-forge-link-to-ancient-kaifeng-community/

[34] http://www.telegraph.co.uk/news/worldnews/asia/china/10776023/China-on-course-to-become-worlds-most-Christian-nation-within-15-years.html

As I have mentioned previously, I believe that this third is in addition to those who have already died in the various environmental disasters that are described in Revelation chapter 8 and which are all described in thirds. Perhaps overall two-thirds of all humanity will perish in accordance with the final outworking of Zechariah 13:8-9. This is great tribulation to say the very least and it is global.

As the Apostle Paul says:

Romans 2:9 (NIV) *There will be trouble and distress for every human being who does evil: first for the Jew, **then for the Gentile*** [emphasis added].

I believe the initial outworking of this Pauline passage has been the possibility that two-thirds of the people of Israel may have perished violently throughout history. They have most certainly drunk from the cup of God's wrath

The Cup of God's Wrath

Isaiah 51:17 (RSV) *Rouse yourself, rouse yourself, stand up, O Jerusalem, **you who have drunk at the hand of the LORD the cup of his wrath*** [emphasis added].

Drinking from this cup accurately reflects the history of the Jewish people. Did they have to drink it? Possibly not, as it is quite likely that this was also the "cup" that Jesus was struggling with in the Garden of Gethsemane.

Mark 14:36 (NIV) *"Abba, Father," he said, "everything is possible for you. Take this cup from me. Yet not what I will, but what you will."*

Jesus knew perfectly well what it was going to cost him to drink from this cup.

But the fact is this: Jesus and the people of Israel have both drunk from this cup, but for them both, at the last, the cup is empty. This expectation is consistent with this passage in Isaiah:

Isaiah 51:22-23 (RSV) *Therefore hear this, you who are afflicted, who are drunk, but not with wine: Thus says your Lord, the LORD, your God who pleads the cause of his people: "Behold, I have taken from your hand the cup of staggering; the bowl of my wrath **you shall drink no more**; **and I will put it into the hand of your tormentors*** [emphasis added].

The passing of the cup of God's wrath to the Gentile nations is also repeated in the prophecy of Jeremiah.

Jeremiah 25:15-16 (NIV) *This is what the LORD, the God of Israel, said to me: "Take from my hand this cup filled with the wine of my wrath and make all the nations to whom I send you drink it. When they drink it, they will stagger and go mad because of the sword I will send among them."*

And perhaps this is also alluded to in Zechariah:

Zechariah 12:2 (NIV) *I am going to make Jerusalem a cup that sends all the surrounding peoples reeling.*

So, maybe, at the last, Jerusalem itself becomes the cup of God's wrath. In fact, I am sure this has been the case since the establishment of the nation in 1948. The survival of the new state of Israel in the War of Independence was nothing short of miraculous. However, perhaps this prophetic expectation has been heightened since the six-day war in 1967. The liberation of Jerusalem and its reunification at that time has brought the city to center stage. But, whatever happens from now on, the city of Jerusalem is here to stay, intact and in its place.

The book of Revelation also speaks of "the cup of God's wrath" in two places. The first one is:

Revelation 14:9-10 (RSV) *And another angel, a third, followed them, saying with a loud voice, "If any one worships the beast and its image, and receives a mark on his forehead or on his hand, he also shall drink **the wine of God's wrath, poured unmixed into the cup of his anger*** [emphasis added].

This is an interesting passage. There is a future aspect as well as a past. The wine of God's fury has already been poured into the cup. In other words, the cup that was drunk by Jesus and the people of Israel has now been re-filled. It will be drunk by all those who submit to the beast whatever that might mean. It is inevitable. Drinking from the cup is also described in chapter 16 following the gathering of the nations at Armageddon.

Revelation 16:17-21 (NIV) *The seventh angel poured out his bowl into the air, and out of the temple came a loud voice from the throne, saying, "It is done!" Then there came flashes of lightning, rumblings, peals of thunder and a severe earthquake. No earthquake like it has ever occurred since man has been on earth, so tremendous was the quake. The great city split into three parts, and the cities of the nations collapsed. God remembered Babylon the Great **and gave her the cup filled with the wine of the fury of his wrath.** Every island fled away and the mountains could not be found. From the sky huge hailstones of about a hundred pounds each fell upon men. And they cursed God on account of the plague of hail, because the plague was so terrible* [emphasis added].

The specific recipient of the cup of God's wrath in this passage is described as Babylon the Great. How are we to identify this city if a city is what it is?

The fall of Babylon the Great, which is alluded to in Revelation 16, is more completely described in Revelation chapter 18. Literally, it is a place of great commerce, perhaps the commercial center of the world but it has become totally corrupt. As a result, all the riches she once had are gone. It is interesting to note that the destruction of this city can be seen from ships afar off.

Revelation 18:17-19 (NIV) *Every sea captain, and all who travel by ship, the sailors, and all who earn their living from the sea, will stand far off. When they see the smoke of her burning, they will exclaim, 'Was there ever a city like this great city?'*

It is tempting to speculate that this is New York City.

Babylon the Great? [35]

At the last, the shaking of the earth will lead to the collapse of many cities across the world. One assumes that it will be worse in those cities packed with skyscrapers. In addition, the "great city" is split into three parts.

---

[35] https://en.wikipedia.org/wiki/Manhattan. I am perfectly aware that there are very many different interpretations of "Mystery Babylon". Some believe that it is Saudi Arabia. Some believe that it will yet be the city of Rome.

It is probable that the "great city" is speaking of Babylon the Great but what is going to initiate this great shaking? I think it may be a cosmic event involving a collision with an extra-planetary object (maybe a giant meteorite). I think this might be alluded to in those prophetic passages that speak of the "stars falling from the sky".[36] Also:

Revelation 8:10-11 (RSV) The third angel blew his trumpet, and a great star fell from heaven, blazing like a torch, and it fell on a third of the rivers and on the fountains of water. The name of the star is Wormwood. A third of the waters became wormwood, and many men died of the water, because it was made bitter.

Revelation 18:21 (RSV) Then a mighty angel took up a stone like a great millstone and threw it into the sea, saying, "So shall Babylon the great city be thrown down with violence, and shall be found no more."

The Judgment of the Nations

The gathering of all the nations to Jerusalem is bringing them step by step towards judgment. As we have already mentioned as the armies approach Jerusalem from the west, at least half of the population of the city are travelling east towards the Mount of Olives. They are certainly being pursued but the Lord is in total control.

Joel 3:1-3 (RSV) For behold, in those days and at that time, when I restore the fortunes of Judah and Jerusalem, I will gather all the nations and bring them down to the valley of Jehoshaphat, and I will enter into judgment with them there, on account of my people and my heritage Israel.

---

[36] **Matthew 24:29 (NIV)** Immediately after the distress of those days "'the sun will be darkened, and the moon will not give its light; the stars will fall from the sky, and the heavenly bodies will be shaken.'

You will have noted that this event is taking place at a time when the Lord has restored the fortunes of Judah and Jerusalem. In addition, he is bringing the advancing armies to a valley called Jehoshaphat which can simply mean "God judges". Is the valley of Jehoshaphat and the great valley that passes through the Mount of Olives, one and the same? There are differences of opinion but all commentators are agreed that it is to the east of Jerusalem, perhaps even the Kidron valley.

Joel 3:11-12 (RSV) Hasten and come, all you nations round about, gather yourselves there. Bring down thy warriors, O LORD. Let the nations bestir themselves, and come up to the valley of Jehoshaphat; for there I will sit to judge all the nations round about.

This is a truly fascinating passage. The armies are gathering in the valley but this is also a trigger point. The cry goes up "Bring down thy warriors, O LORD". Who is speaking? It is obviously not the Lord. It must be the people of Israel who are acting in faith. The warriors are God's mighty angels.

And so several things are taking place at the same time.

1. His feet are standing on the Mount of Olives
2. A great valley is created that will enable the people of Israel to flee to safety.
3. The angelic host "comes down" to make battle with the armies that have attacked Jerusalem
4. These armies have been brought into a trap from which there is no escape.

Joel 3:16 (RSV) **And** *the LORD roars from Zion, and ut-ters his voice from Jerusalem, and the heavens and the earth shake.* **But the LORD is a refuge to his people, a stronghold to the people of Israel** [emphases added].

I hope you noted the words "and" and "but". In the midst of all this battle between the nations of the world and the angelic host, the nation of Israel is still safe. The Lord is a stronghold and a refuge for his people. One might even argue that the inhabitants of Jerusalem have to be evacuated from the city before this final conflict. The Lord has provided a way of escape through the valley.

The Valley of Jehoshaphat

Have you ever thought why the valley of judgment is called the Valley of Jehoshaphat? We have already considered the meaning of the name which is simply "God judges" or perhaps more accurately "God has judged". But is this the only reason? The valley is also named after one of the kings of Judah. We read about him in 2 Chronicles chapter 17.

2 Chronicles 17:3 (NKJV) *Now the LORD was with Jehoshaphat, because he walked in the former ways of his father David.*

Sadly, at the beginning of his reign, Jehoshaphat made an alliance with Ahab, king of the northern Kingdom of Israel, that proved disastrous. The prophet Jehu challenged him.

2 Chronicles19:1-3 (NKJV) *Then Jehoshaphat the king of Judah returned safely to his house in Jerusalem. And Jehu the son of Hanani the seer went out to meet him, and said to King Jehoshaphat, "Should you help the wicked and love those who hate the LORD? Therefore the wrath of the LORD is upon you. Nevertheless good things are found in you, in that you have removed the wooden images from the land, and have prepared your heart to seek God."*

Jehoshaphat had learned his lesson. He encouraged the people of Judah to return to the Lord. This commitment, however, was soon to be tested when the nation came under attack.

__2 Chronicles 20:2-4 (NKJV)__ Some came and told Jehoshaphat, saying, "A great multitude is coming against you from beyond the sea, from Syria … And Jehoshaphat feared, and set himself to seek the LORD, and proclaimed a fast throughout all Judah. So Judah gathered together to ask help from the LORD; and from all the cities of Judah they came to seek the LORD.

In the midst of this gathering, Jehoshaphat prays and he concludes his prayer with these words.

__2 Chronicles 20:12 (NKJV)__ O our God, __will You not judge them?__ For we have no power against this great multitude that is coming against us; nor do we know what to do, but our eyes are upon You [emphasis added].

In response to the prayers and the fasting, another prophet named Jahaziel encourages them to remain steadfast.

__2 Chronicles 20:17 (NKJV)__ You will not need to fight in this battle. Position yourselves, stand still and see the salvation of the LORD, who is with you, O Judah and Jerusalem!' Do not fear or be dismayed; tomorrow go out against them, for the LORD is with you."

It is extremely significant, therefore, that we reconsider and compare the exhortation of Moses to the people of Israel at the crossing of the sea, namely,

__Exodus 14:13-14 (RSV)__ And Moses said to the people, "Fear not, stand firm, and see the salvation of the LORD, which he will work for you today; for the Egyptians whom you see today, you shall never see again. The LORD will fight for you, and you have only to be still."

The parallel is no coincidence.

Subsequently, Jehoshaphat appointed some of the people to sing and praise the Lord.[37] They went ahead of the army and the enemy was defeated. Thus, I believe that, as in the days of the Exodus, as in the days of Jehoshaphat, during the final battle, the Lord will be in total control. Will it be safe? Yes, I believe it will. As the Lord says in Joel:

Joel 3:17-18 (RSV) *So you shall know that I am the LORD your God, who dwell in Zion, my holy mountain and Jerusalem shall be holy and strangers shall never again pass through it. And in that day the mountains shall drip sweet wine, and the hills shall flow with milk, and all the stream beds of Judah shall flow with water; and a fountain shall come forth from the house of the LORD.[38]*

And as we will see, these dramatic changes are consistent with other passages in the prophetic scriptures.

Geological Changes in Israel in the Last Days

The prophets speak of significant geological and geographical changes taking place in Israel in the last days.

Isaiah 2:2 (RSV) *It shall come to pass in the latter days that the mountain of the house of the LORD shall be established as the highest of the mountains, and shall be raised above the hills; and all the nations shall flow to it.*

Isaiah 40:4-5 (RSV) *Every valley shall be lifted up, and every mountain and hill be made low; the uneven ground shall become level, and the rough places a plain. And the glory of the LORD shall be revealed, and all flesh shall see it together, for the mouth of the LORD has spoken.*

---

[37] **2 Chronicles 20:21 (NIV)** After consulting the people, Jehoshaphat appointed men to sing to the LORD and to praise him for the splendor of his holiness as they went out at the head of the army, saying: "Give thanks to the LORD, for his love endures forever." This refrain is also to be found at the beginning and end of Psalm 118.

[38] See also Ezekiel chapter 47

Zechariah 14:10 (NIV) *Jerusalem will be raised up and remain in its place.*

All of these prophetic passages seem to indicate that the great shaking that devastates the world will also have profound geological effects in Israel. In particular, we know that a fault line runs through the Mount of Olives. We have already considered the prophecy of Zechariah describing what happens when the Lord returns to the city and stands on this hill. The great valley that will be created through what is now the Mount of Olives will allow many (perhaps half the population of Jerusalem) to flee for safety from the advancing armies in the final battle.

This geological activity will also release an unbelievable volume of subterranean water.

Zechariah 14:8 (NIV) *On that day living water will flow out from Jerusalem, half to the eastern sea and half to the western sea, in summer and in winter.*

Among other things, at least part of the African Rift Valley will be supplied with vast quantities of fresh water. The Dead Sea will no longer be dead.

Ezekiel 47:10-12 (RSV) *Fishermen will stand beside the sea; from En-gedi to En-eglaim it will be a place for the spreading of nets; its fish will be of very many kinds, like the fish of the Great Sea. But its swamps and marshes will not become fresh; they are to be left for salt. And on the banks, on both sides of the river, there will grow all kinds of trees for food. Their leaves will not wither nor their fruit fail, but they will bear fresh fruit every month, because the water for them flows from the sanctuary. Their fruit will be for food, and their leaves for healing.*

Thus, the water that floods the land will also cause the desert to blossom as described in many other prophetic passages. For example,

Isaiah 51:3 (NIV) *The LORD will surely comfort Zion and will look with compassion on all her ruins; he will make her deserts like Eden, her wastelands like the garden of the LORD. Joy and gladness will be found in her, thanksgiving and the sound of singing.*

The King is Coming Back

Revelation 19:11-16 (RSV) *Then I saw heaven opened, and behold, a white horse! He who sat upon it is called Faithful and True, and in righteousness he judges and makes war. His eyes are like a flame of fire, and on his head are many diadems; and he has a name inscribed which no one knows but himself. He is clad in a robe dipped in blood, and the name by which he is called is The Word of God. And the armies of heaven, arrayed in fine linen, white and pure, followed him on white horses. From his mouth issues a sharp sword with which to smite the nations, and he will rule them with a rod of iron; he will tread the wine press of the fury of the wrath of God the Almighty. On his robe and on his thigh he has a name inscribed, King of kings and Lord of lords.*

Zechariah 14:9 (NIV) *The LORD will be king over the whole earth. On that day there will be one LORD, and his name the only name.*

As we have seen, in the midst of the final battle, the Lord comes to fight against those nations that he has gathered. He comes with all his holy ones including the angelic host (the armies of heaven). This event is also described by the Apostle Paul in his second letter to the Thessalonians.

2 Thessalonians 1:7-10 (NIV) *This will happen when the Lord Jesus is revealed from heaven in blazing fire with his powerful angels. He will punish those who do not know God and do not obey the gospel of our Lord Jesus. They will be punished with everlasting destruction and shut out from the presence of the Lord and from the majesty of his power on the day he comes to be glorified in his holy people and to be marveled at among all those who have believed. This includes you, because you believed our testimony to you.*

Thus, the "holy ones" will also include believers from all over the earth. Those who have died will be raised and those who are alive will be changed in the twinkling of an eye.

Matthew 24:30-31 (RSV) *Then will appear the sign of the Son of man in heaven, and then all the tribes of the earth will mourn, and they will see the Son of man coming on the clouds of heaven with power and great glory; and he will send out his angels with a loud trumpet call, and they will gather his elect from the four winds, from one end of heaven to the other.*

This is the Lord's own word as the Apostle Paul reminds us:

1 Thessalonians 4:14-18 (NIV) *We believe that Jesus died and rose again and so we believe that God will bring with Jesus those who have fallen asleep in him. According to the Lord's own word, we tell you that we who are still alive, who are left till the coming of the Lord, **will certainly not precede those who have fallen asleep.** For the Lord himself will come down from heaven, with a loud command, with the voice of the archangel and with the trumpet call of God, and the dead in Christ will rise **first. After that,** we who are still alive and are left will be caught up together with them in the clouds to meet the Lord in the air. **And so we will be with the Lord forever*** [emphases added].

Whatever the "rapture" means, it will take place after the resurrection of the dead which is at the return of Jesus. It is the gathering of the elect – not into heavenly places – but to be with the Lord forever. And where will the Lord be forever? He will reign in Jerusalem.

Ezekiel 43:7 (NIV) *He said: "Son of man, this is the place of my throne and the place for the soles of my feet.* ***This is where I will live among the Israelites forever*** [emphasis added].

Joel 3:20-21 (NIV) *Judah will be **inhabited forever** and **Jerusalem through all generations.** Their bloodguilt, which I have not pardoned, I will pardon.' **The LORD dwells in Zion*** [emphases added].

In my opinion, the "rapture" is simply angelic transportation to Jerusalem! No-one, no believer alive or who has died will want to miss this event. And they won't! And there will be a place for us there as well.

John 14:1-3 (NIV) *Do not let your hearts be troubled. Trust in God; trust also in me. In my Father's house are many rooms; if it were not so, I would have told you. I am going there to prepare a place for you. And if I go and prepare a place for you, **I will come back and take you to be with me that you also may be where I am*** [emphasis added].

Yes, the final events of this age are going to be extremely difficult. But as Jesus says:

Revelation 22:20-21 (NIV) *"Yes, I am coming soon."*

Amen. Come, Lord Jesus. The grace of the Lord Jesus be with God's people. Amen.